2:17 a.m.

Debbie Tam

BookLeaf Publishing

India | USA | UK

Presentation by *BookLeaf Publishing*

Web: www.bookleafpub.com

E-mail: info@bookleafpub.com

ISBN: 9789360949693

First edition 2024

Open 24 Hours

The faint hum of the overhead fluorescent lights
Like the flight tone of the fly
The bitterness of a scorched coffee pot waiting
Just beyond the swinging doors
A cook stands ready in
This city's penumbric refuge
For the restless seeking familiarity
For those seeking warmth one mug at a time
For those when last call moves the need for
amaranthine mischief
To sober prospects and disco fries
The congregation recedes when the eggs begin
to sizzle.

His Love

He pretends not to notice
When she rises
For the second time this night
Sheets rustling
She heads to the bathroom
Slippers shuffling

He pretends not to notice
Her hair that first caught his eye
An ebony crown
Grown thin now with intermittent gray
As she struggles to cover it with a scarf

He pretends not to notice
The chin hairs
That she plucks secretly
Usually too late
Angry wiry things
That only make him laugh

He pretends not to notice
Her steps have grown slower
Her knees protest at a flight of stairs
Her hands are cold when he clasps them

He pretends not to notice
Anything inevitable

HEAR Report

"County General, this is Jane in Ambulance 12."
Who is on her second cup of coffee of the night
Hoping Shondra studied for her geometry test
Took this shift because it pays more
Sleeps during the day like a vampire
Whose mother reminds her she could have been
a doctor if she didn't let Wilson put a baby in her

"We are en route with a 67-year-old male."
Who reminds her of her father
That worked two jobs
Who was a ghost who haunted their home
Where hellos replaced meaningful connections
Retired now
A man she barely knows

"Patient complains of chest pain."
Jane aches from her head to her toes
Dreaming of vacations she will never take
Of sandy shores and fruity drinks
Denied because of sensible decisions
Like rent and food

"9 out of 10. Pain began one hour ago."
Pain starts at the soul

Radiating to her jaws
Trapping a scream she can't release
From a kind of tired that sleep can't cure
For Shondra, she tells herself

"ASA and Nitro administered. Chest pain
relieved."
Simple solutions in the rig
Another life saved
If only life had
Neatly labeled drawers
Training with rigid steps
Flashing lights and warning sirens
Her pulse slows
As she squeezes his hand

"ETA, 8 minutes."
Jane rubs her neck
As she files her report
Succinct details of a death thwarted
Carl blows through red lights
The siren wails like a banshee through the
streets
While people sleep

"Questions or orders?"
Orders are easy.
Questions are hard.

Night Wakings

5

Almost a dream
A snatch of something
Quickly fading now
As the baby's cry
Forces her heavy lids open
She stumbles into the rocking chair
Plucking her breast out
Slowly his eyes close
Slowly her eyes close
Both contented

Her Love

He thinks he's a sly fox
That I don't know I wake him up every night
But does he know
It's his snoring that gets me up
Sure, nature calls
But it wouldn't be ringing
If not for his snuffling
And he wakes me
Grabbing at the covers
Leaving me shivering
Then there's the tossing and turning
And odd elbow jab
That would wake anyone up
Linda says I should sleep in the guest room
Sure, I might get more sleep
But I wouldn't sleep better

Missed

Surprising life at Terminal B
Watching lucky scuttling travelers
Catching red-eyes
But not me
You made me late for my flight
With words dripping bitterness
Consuming gravity
Chewing minutes
Then an hour
As my ride pulled away
Then the tears came next
Trite rehearsed remorse
Objective achieved
So now I sit
In Terminal B
Waiting for the next flight
Wishing I didn't have to return

Jackpot

These are the desperate hours
The spangled cocktail servers
Barely get a glance
Despite the exposed thighs
And spilling cleavage
These are not the people of sunlight
Lighthearted, passing by on a lark
Or the thrillseekers in the early evening
Channeling Monte Carlo romance
These people exchange sleep with misguided
hope
That comes in whirling colors and provocative
chimes
With promises that fortune may turn
In another hour or two
And if not, at least the drinks are free.

Nature of the Emergency

"911. State the nature of the emergency."
"My father collapsed. I think it's a heart attack."

Please let this be the end.
Three miserable years as his life drags on
Those dull gray eyes judging me for a lifetime

"How old is your father?"
"67 years old."

Thirty some odd years at the plant
Reminding me and my mother
How we should be brimming with gratitude
As he pawed her exhausted yet yielding body
With her eyes glistening with contempt

"What is your name?"
"Edith Spencer."

That Edith who showed up to school
In ill-fitting clothes
Cast-offs like herself
That Edith who bore the cruelty of children
Nothing compared to what she received at home

"Where are you located?"
"183 Oak Lane."

That ninth circle of hell
That I nearly clawed my way out
Chasing skyscrapers
Until that phone call snapped me back
To this neutral toned dungeon
With shag carpeting

"Is he breathing?"
"Yes."

Why did I call?
Is it too late to smother him with a pillow?

"Please stay on the line. Emergency personnel
have been dispatched to your location."

Always the good daughter.
I hate myself.

Haunted

I am more than an eyesore
This composite of wood and brick and shattered
glass
I'm the subject of gossip
That place where so-and-so committed that
sinister deed
That somehow never made it in the papers
Or the history books
Or saw the inside of a courtroom
And yet the oft-told tale is repeated
Like a solemn hymn
Creating a truth
That begs teenaged sorties
Of rocks and spray paint
I was once a home
A family's dream, bristling with love
Until abandoned
They say I am haunted
They are not wrong

Enjoy Your Stay

They come bleary-eyed
From the other side of the world
Talking loudly in English
Over-enunciating each syllable
Like I am slow
With a welcoming grin
I'll play along
An ingratiating host
For your home for the week
As you buy overpriced souvenirs
Post photos of crumbling landmarks
We need your dollars
So enjoy your stay

Dream

He's here with me every night
Perfectly rendered
Down to that spot he always missed shaving
Just inside that cleft in his chin
In the shirt he wore
When we were married at city hall
I'm never alone
In this dream on repeat

Fall In

I'm a good father
Tuck my boys in bed every night
With a story of happy endings
They've outgrown it
Though they don't have the heart to let on
Those yawns aren't just about drowsiness
But I'll keep reading if they keep listening
They know the rules
Once the lights go off
They don't leave the beds
Business is being conducted
Through the kitchen window
Busier as the night wears on
This is no one's dream
But my boys want for nothing

Please Don't Vomit in My Cab

I'm not your priest
Don't explain that you broke a promise to
yourself
That you saw him tonight
That man who swears he'll leave his wife
But never does
I'm just trapped with you
And your sour stench of regret
My meter is not implied consent
To vomit your soul

Still Worth It

Hours past curfew
She expects to find her mother
Scowl of disappointment on her face
Toll to be paid
Still worth it
As she smiles to herself
Remembering the taste of Ruby on her lips

Nightmare

It's just enough your town
That when it begins
Just strolling known landscapes
Until you turn an unfamiliar corner
Then the chase begins
You don't turn
You don't need to see it
You feel it
Steps thundering at your heels
Or maybe it's the other one
Where you are falling
Falling
Falling
Never landing
Or it's the one where you're standing naked
Or the one where all your teeth fall out
No matter
You won't remember it anyway

Spin Cycle

Watching colors tumble
To the drone of the television
Frozen on a news channel
Spilling doom
Captive until that buzz
Then the fresh smell of linens
Warm like rolls from an oven

Corridors

Nothing happy comes through those doors
In the dark hours
One takes inventory of a life
Bringing a frantic urgency
Exposing raw nerves
Some come with families
Most come alone
Knowing this place intimately
Not the first go-around
These corridors have heard
Screams from invisible terrors
Wailing from unshakeable sorrow
Silence from an insatiable hollow
We offer safety
But healing begins beyond our doors

Fallout

I know this house
With two little boys
One rides his shiny bike around town
A little reckless
I've warned him to watch for traffic
But his ears are clogged with music
And he waves me off
The other boy
Is in my daughter's class
I've seen him at concerts
Lips moving
Though I doubt he's singing
Just two ordinary boys
Neatly dressed
Well-fed
Probably well-loved
Sure, why not
Law-abiding citizens don't have a monopoly on
love
Their eyes burn through me
As I cuff their father

Night Musings in Study Carrel Number32

In study carrel number 32
My wanders from the accounting text in front of
me
Of my parents who came here 22 years ago
My father worked as a waiter for most of his life
Making money under the table
Learning English on the fly
Selling real estate in his few precious free hours
My mother made me her life's work
No time for play
Each minute rationed for study, violin, and
ballet.
Friends were a distraction
My mother wore my grades like a badge
I'm fighting for the next one now
Longing for bed while I stuff one more useless
fact in my brain
To get a job that they will approve
When I dream of mixing drinks at a resort

Desynchronosis

A late-night touchdown
In a foreign city
Seven messages from her
The evident panic rising
While I slept on the plane
First came anger
Accusations of desertion
Because my company sent me here
Next came sadness
Longing for my presence
Then back to anger
Because we couldn't afford a ticket for her
But the worst was the fear
The dread in her voice
Of being alone

Despite the punishing time change
Relief comes from the blessed chime
As my magnetic key card
Opens the door effortlessly on the first try
Small blessings

Staring at Cracks

I can hear everything
Creaking floors that shriek
As the mother upstairs pounds the hardwoods
With the newborn who goes off like an alarm
Then the rocking like a booming pendulum
Next a siren splits the silent streets
And fades off but not until my heart bolts from
my chest
But none of this the true cause
Why I can't sleep
Something gnawing
Nibbling the corners of my brain
A pestilence of second guesses
A reel of redux of perfect replies
As I lie here, eyes pointed to the ceiling
Staring at cracks